The EVOLUTION of a HEALED WOMAN!

The Journey into Freedom!

Six-week Spiritual Journal Workbook

PIVOTING INTO PURPOSE · PIVOTING INTO PURPOSE · PIVOTING INTO PURPOSE · PIVOTING INTO PURPOSE

Dedication

To the one who made me realize that falling in love was still possible.

Thank you for the experience.

Acknowledgments

There are so many people to thank for being an inspiration to this project. Thank you to everyone who has believed in me and my ministry. Thank you for your words of wisdom and always speaking life into the visions that God deposits into my spirt.

Thank you to the contributors to this journal.

Valentina Alexandre'

Treasure Griffin

Jamie Ralliford AKA Ms. Chu

Aisha Marie Jackson

Parvathi Kumar Photography

Yves- Andre Innocent

Designhillbd

Forward

The day I met Whitney Smith, I had been very nervous to be entering a new space altogether. I was a potential member of her school team, guided to visit her classroom because she was deemed by the school's principal to be an exceptional leader, author, pastor, and educator. I had been star-struck walking in to see this confident Black woman, floating around the room in her heels as if on clouds, gathering data from her quiet and engaged pupils. My first impression was that she is respected.

When I joined the team, I was assigned to co-teach with Whitney, and the man in me was intimidated. Her content knowledge of writing was incredible, I was learning things I never learned before from her. What took me off guard, however, was how authentic and down-to-earth Whitney was. She carried a certain joy about her, always smiling when she taught, easily admitting to her students when she made errors, unafraid and unapologetic about her humanity. That is what drew me to get to know her even beyond the workplace. And we got close.

Whitney Smith is one of the most authentic, inspiring, proactive, and ambitious people that I know. She is driven by her greater purpose and so her impact is deeply felt by those who come into contact with her and her work. Whitney Smith has dedicated a large portion of her life post-trauma to healing herself and those around her. She has led countless self-development workshops and conferences where women have come out on the other side with a sense of clarity on how to connect to their source, on how to be decisive about their life's purpose and goals, and on how to take action to make their dream lives a reality.

In fact, through her work, I have seen so many others thrive, start businesses, open up to their families and friends, seek growth, and more. Her reach is immeasurable. This journal that she has put together is the genesis of her own healing journey. In her reflectiveness, Whitney Smith has gone inward to demystify the path and steps that she has taken to arrive at her own healing in order to make it clear and accessible for all through this journal.

It is both mine and her hope that this journal supports you to begin your own journey to healing and clarity. This is a gift. Use it. Apply it. Pay it forward.

Valentina Alexandre

Promissory Note

This promissory note is a promise to yourself and your journey to allow yourself to be what you need to be to create and fall into you without apologizing. Read the promises and then add your own. Many people break their promises. Do not break your promises to you.

- » I promise to give myself the space to enjoy myself.
- » I promise to give myself the freedom to spend time with my emotions.
- » I promise to allow myself to feel.
- » I promise to allow myself to reflect on how much progress I made in my journal.
- » I promise to be real with myself.
- » I promise not to judge myself for the choices and decisions I made in my past.
- » I promise to love on myself.
- » I promise to use this journal to create time for me to grow, heal, and discover.
- » I promise to give myself grace if I become distracted and off track.
- » I promise to give myself permission to learn some interesting things about myself.
- » I promise to allow myself to heal.
- » I promise not to beat myself up.
- » I promise to talk nice to myself.
- » I promise to choose me.

This is a promissory agreement between who I am now and the higher version of myself who is excited to meet me.

My Signature

YOU ARE *purpose*

Is It A Truth or A lie?

Many of us have been subjected to the words, feelings, and emotions of others. Many of us have experienced others projecting how they feel about themselves on us, which has scared us emotionally into believing certain things about ourselves that are certainly not true. We have accepted these beliefs as facts; accepted these things as truths, which has hindered our transformation and growth into becoming the best version of ourselves. In this practice below, write down what people have told you that you accepted as a fact or a truth, cross it out, then write down what God says about you. What God says about you is the truth, not what others say about you.

Lie

....

What does God say about you?

....

....

Lie

....

What does God say about you?

....

....

Lie

....

What does God say about you?

....

....

Lie

....

What does God say about you?

....

....

Lie

....

What does God say about you?

....

....

Trust in the Lord

Trust in the LORD with all your heart and lean not on your own understanding; in all your ways submit to him, and he will make your paths straight

(Proverbs 3:5-7)

Heavenly Father, there are times where I lean on my own understanding and that is when I become doubtful, fearful, and not trusting the journey of the process. I sometimes get in my own way because I lean on what I see, I lean on what's around me, I lean on other people's opinions, I lean on distractions, and I sometimes lean on what is not serving you. Heavenly father today, I submit to you every part of me, every area of my life, and all my desires. Please order my thoughts and order my steps, so I can see clearly and become who you are calling me to be, in Jesus' name, Amen.

Week 1

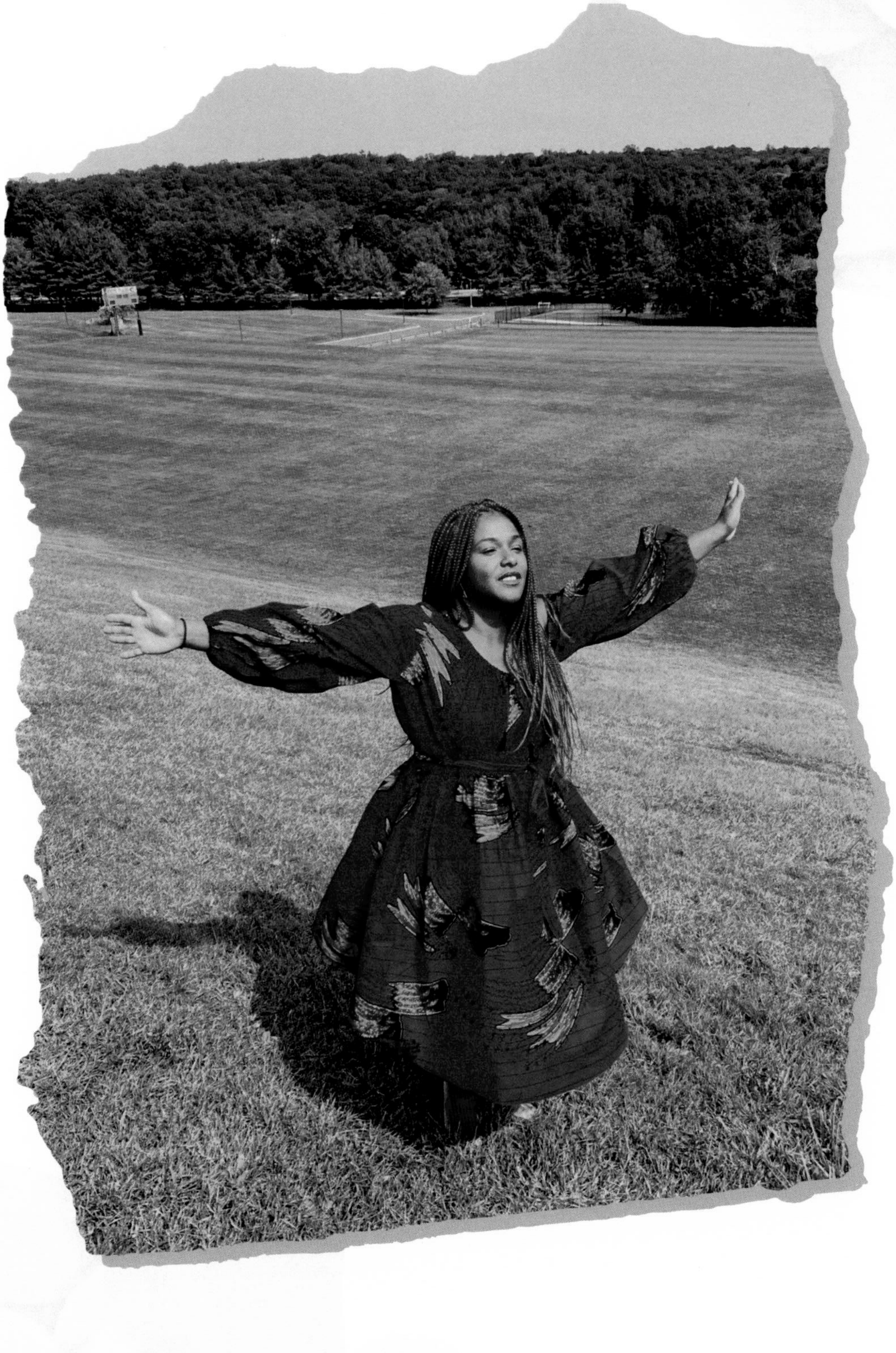

You are NEVER too old! & It's NEVER too late!

Date: _____

I am grateful for...

_____

○ ....

My prayer for today...

_____

....

....

My song for today...

_____

○ ....

My scripture for today...

_____

....

My personal goals I am declaring today...

_____

○ ....

○ ....

Actions that I will commit to today that will align me with my personal goals...

_____

○ ....

○ ....

The daily affirmations that will serve me today...

_____

○ ....

○ ....

I am grateful for...

My prayer for today...

My song for today...

My scripture for today...

My personal goals I am declaring today...

Actions that I will commit to today that will align me with my personal goals...

The daily affirmations that will serve me today...

I am grateful for...

....

○ ....

My prayer for today...

....

....

My song for today...

○ ....

My scripture for today...

....

My personal goals I am declaring today...

....

○ ....

Actions that I will commit to today that will align me with my personal goals...

○ ....

○ ....

The daily affirmations that will serve me today...

○ ....

○ ....

Date: _____

I am grateful for...

_____

My prayer for today...

_____

My song for today...

My scripture for today...

_____

My personal goals I am declaring today...

_____

Actions that I will commit to today that will align me with my personal goals...

_____

The daily affirmations that will serve me today...

_____

I am grateful for...

My prayer for today...

My song for today...

My scripture for today...

My personal goals I am declaring today...

Actions that I will commit to today that will align me with my personal goals...

The daily affirmations that will serve me today...

Weekly Self-Reflection
Practice 1

1. Reread your journal entry.
   Describe the emotions and thoughts that are present during and after your reading.

   ....

   ....

   ....

2. Describe at least one distraction that you may have encountered during the week. How did you handle it? Did it hold you back from staying focused on accomplishing your weekly goals?

   ....

   ....

   ....

3. What behaviors will you change from the previous week that will propel you into the new week?

   ....

   ....

Week 2

YOU BELONG HERE!

For I know the plans I have for you, declares the Lord, plans to prosper you and not to harm you, plans to give you hope and a future

Jeremiah 29:11

Thank you, God, for creating me for a purpose even when I have struggled and wrestled to know exactly what my purpose may be. I may still struggle, however, what I do know is that the plans you have for me are bigger than I could ever imagine. I am trusting that I can be secure in that thought because of who you are. I know I belong here. I know no matter what my circumstances feel or look like, I belong here. You have created me to manifest the visions that you have deposited into me. I find hope in you. I find hope in the fact that I do not have to have it all figured out because of who you are. I belong to you, and in that belonging to you, I know I will prosper in the plans that you have for me, in Jesus' name, Amen.

Date: _____

I am grateful for…

_____

My prayer for today…

_____

_____

My song for today…

My scripture for today…

_____

My personal goals I am declaring today…

_____

_____

Actions that I will commit to today that will align me with my personal goals…

_____

The daily affirmations that will serve me today…

_____

Date: _____

I am grateful for...

My prayer for today...

My song for today...

My scripture for today...

My personal goals I am declaring today...

Actions that I will commit to today that will align me with my personal goals...

The daily affirmations that will serve me today...

I am grateful for…

My prayer for today…

My song for today…

My scripture for today…

My personal goals I am declaring today…

Actions that I will commit to today that will align me with my personal goals…

The daily affirmations that will serve me today…

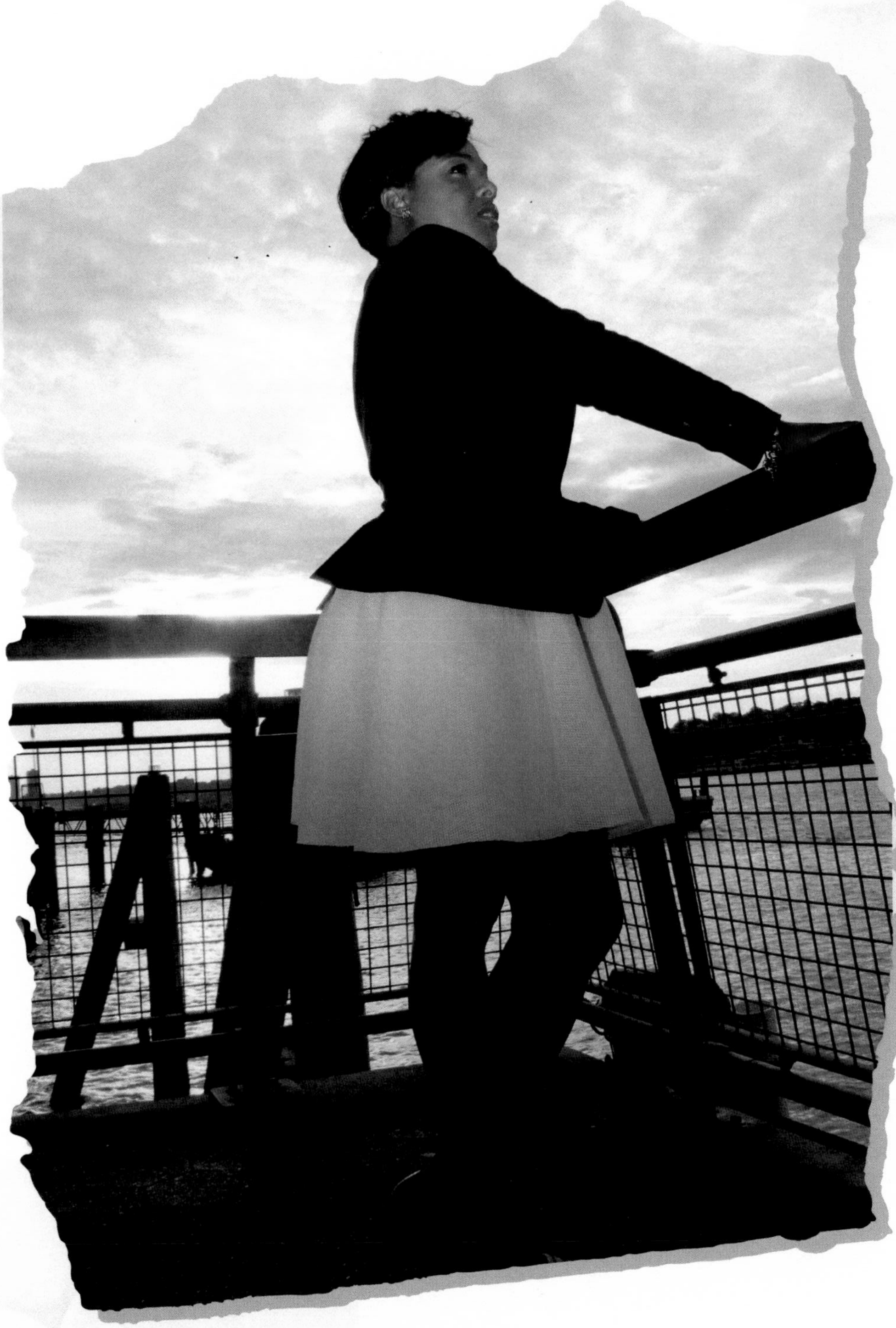

You Can't BE What

You Can't See!

—Marian Wright Edelman

Date: _____

I am grateful for...

My prayer for today...

My song for today...

My scripture for today...

My personal goals I am declaring today...

Actions that I will commit to today that will align me with my personal goals...

The daily affirmations that will serve me today...

I am grateful for...

My prayer for today...

My song for today...

My scripture for today...

My personal goals I am declaring today...

Actions that I will commit to today that will align me with my personal goals...

The daily affirmations that will serve me today...

I am grateful for...

_____

_____

My prayer for today...

_____

_____

_____

My song for today...

_____

My scripture for today...

_____

_____

My personal goals I am declaring today...

_____

_____

Actions that I will commit to today that will align me with my personal goals...

_____

_____

The daily affirmations that will serve me today...

_____

Date: _____

I am grateful for...

My prayer for today...

My song for today...

My scripture for today...

My personal goals I am declaring today...

Actions that I will commit to today that will align me with my personal goals...

The daily affirmations that will serve me today...

Weekly Self-Reflection
Practice 2

1. Reread your journal entry.
Describe the emotions and thoughts that are present during and after your reading.

2. Describe at least one distraction that you may have encountered during the week. How did you handle it? Did it hold you back from staying focused on accomplishing your weekly goals?

3. What behaviors will you change from the previous week that will propel you into the new week?

Week 3

Don't Worry!

Do not boast about tomorrow,
for you do not know what a day may bring

(Proverbs 27:1)

Dear Lord,

I will not think about what tomorrow will bring. Tomorrow has its own comings. I will lay my thoughts on tomorrow in your hands. I will be present for today and be thankful for this day that you have given me. I will take advantage of this day because you have blessed me to be able to wake up this morning. Today will be a great day because you are with me, in Jesus' name, Amen!

Date: _____

I am grateful for...

My prayer for today...

My song for today...

My scripture for today...

My personal goals I am declaring today...

Actions that I will commit to today that will align me with my personal goals...

The daily affirmations that will serve me today...

I am grateful for...

My prayer for today...

My song for today...

My scripture for today...

My personal goals I am declaring today...

Actions that I will commit to today that will align me with my personal goals...

The daily affirmations that will serve me today...

Date: _____

I am grateful for...

My prayer for today...

My song for today...

My scripture for today...

My personal goals I am declaring today...

Actions that I will commit to today that will align me with my personal goals...

The daily affirmations that will serve me today...

Yesterday, IS WHAT IT WAS....

Yesterday!

Yesterday!

Say Yes To TO-DAY!

I am grateful for...

My prayer for today...

My song for today...

My scripture for today...

My personal goals I am declaring today...

Actions that I will commit to today that will align me with my personal goals...

The daily affirmations that will serve me today...

Date:

Date: _____

I am grateful for...

My prayer for today...

My song for today...

My scripture for today...

My personal goals I am declaring today...

Actions that I will commit to today that will align me with my personal goals...

The daily affirmations that will serve me today...

I am grateful for...

My prayer for today...

My song for today...

My scripture for today...

My personal goals I am declaring today...

Actions that I will commit to today that will align me with my personal goals...

The daily affirmations that will serve me today...

Date: _____

I am grateful for...

My prayer for today...

My song for today...

My scripture for today...

My personal goals I am declaring today...

Actions that I will commit to today that will align me with my personal goals...

The daily affirmations that will serve me today...

Weekly Self-Reflection
Practice 3

1. Reread your journal entry.
   Describe the emotions and thoughts that are present during and after your reading.

2. Describe at least one distraction that you may have encountered during the week. How did you handle it? Did it hold you back from staying focused on accomplishing your weekly goals?

3. What behaviors will you change from the previous week that will propel you into the new week?

Week 4

What Do You See?

66

Then the Lord replied "Write the vision; make it plain on tablets, so he may run who reads it

(Habakkuk 2:2)

Dear God,

Please deposit the visions and your desires into my heart. What is it that you have for me? How would you like me to serve your kingdom here on earth? God, I want to be ALL you created me to be and use my talents and gifts for your glory. I know you created me to live abundantly, to create marvelous things, and to connect people back to you. God, work in me and show me the visions you have for me. Lord, I do not want to go to the grave full of purpose, dreams, books, and businesses. I want to be empty when I come back to you. Thank you, God, for clearing the space, so I can see the visions and the steps that I need to take to fulfill the plans you have for me, in Jesus' name, I pray, Amen.

Practice:

ψ Listen to soft instrumental music

ψ Close your eyes and daydream

ψ Open your eyes

ψ Write down what you see

Start your sentence with I see, I feel, and/or I taste.

ψ I see myself _____

ψ I see myself _____

ψ I see myself _____

ψ I feel myself _____

ψ I feel myself _____

ψ I taste _____

ψ I taste _____

On the next page, create what you see, feel, and/or taste. Cut out images, words, and add pictures of your vision.

Create your
Vision...

Healing Through Serving

66

*LORD my God, I called to you for help,
and you healed me.*

(Psalm 30:2)

The Men's Ministry at my church was having its Annual Father's Day fish fry in conjunction with celebrating the new national holiday Juneteenth. I really didn't want to attend because I was experiencing the pain of loss and my heart was aching. I wasn't in the mood to speak to anyone and pretend as if I was ok with a fake smile. I decided to go anyway because I wanted to support the ministry. I arrived at the event, put on my happy and content mask, and started to have mini conversations with everyone who was in attendance. One of the men came over to me and asked me to bless the food and to help with the prayer session. I really wanted to say, "Can you ask someone else?" However, I didn't because I was called to minister and again, I am an Associate Minister at my church, so I couldn't say no. I said, "Sure!" I went to cover the prayer session and served through my hurt and pain. Many people came to me for prayer. As I was ministering and serving the people, God was ministering to me. My sister in ministry who was with me at the prayer session put her hand on my forehead and prayed to God on my behalf. I needed to cover the prayer session that day because God knew exactly what I needed before I needed it. God positioned me to minister and serve in my pain to remind me although life was tough and I was hurt, He was with me. I became stronger in my pain that day. I immediately knew that God heard me and wasn't going to let me experience my hurt alone.

Do not stop serving when you are experiencing rough life: keep serving God and God's people. You will find your healing and God will meet you exactly where you are.

Lord,

You know exactly what I need before I know what I need. God, thank you for meeting me where I am. Thank you for my healing. Thank you for hearing me when my soul cries out to you. I will serve through my pain to receive my healing, in the name of Jesus, Amen.

I am grateful for...

_____

_____

My prayer for today...

_____

_____

My song for today...

_____

My scripture for today...

_____

_____

My personal goals I am declaring today...

_____

_____

Actions that I will commit to today that will align me with my personal goals...

_____

_____

The daily affirmations that will serve me today...

_____

_____

I am grateful for...

My prayer for today...

My song for today...

My scripture for today...

My personal goals I am declaring today...

Actions that I will commit to today that will align me with my personal goals...

The daily affirmations that will serve me today...

I am grateful for...

My prayer for today...

My song for today...

My scripture for today...

My personal goals I am declaring today...

Actions that I will commit to today that will align me with my personal goals...

The daily affirmations that will serve me today...

If You Didn't Have A TEST *You Wouldn't* Have A TESTIMONY!

I am grateful for...

My prayer for today...

My song for today...

My scripture for today...

My personal goals I am declaring today...

Actions that I will commit to today that will align me with my personal goals...

The daily affirmations that will serve me today...

Date: _____

I am grateful for...

_____

_____

My prayer for today...

_____

_____

_____

My song for today...

_____

My scripture for today...

_____

_____

My personal goals I am declaring today...

_____

_____

Actions that I will commit to today that will align me with my personal goals...

_____

_____

The daily affirmations that will serve me today...

_____

_____

Date: _____

I am grateful for...

___
○ ○ ○

My prayer for today...

My song for today...
○

My scripture for today...

My personal goals I am declaring today...
○ ○

Actions that I will commit to today that will align me with my personal goals...
○ ○

The daily affirmations that will serve me today...
○ ○ ○

Date: _____

I am grateful for…

My prayer for today…

My song for today…

My scripture for today…

My personal goals I am declaring today…

Actions that I will commit to today that will align me with my personal goals…

The daily affirmations that will serve me today…

Weekly Self-Reflection
Practice 4

1. Reread your journal entry.
   Describe the emotions and thoughts that are present during and after your reading.

   ....

   ....

   ....

2. Describe at least one distraction that you may have encountered during the week. How did you handle it? Did it hold you back from staying focused on accomplishing your weekly goals?

   ....

   ....

   ....

3. What behaviors will you change from the previous week that will propel you into the new week?

   ....

   ....

   ....

Week 5

GOD IS A PROMISE KEEPER

And thus Abraham, having patiently waited, obtained the promise

(Hebrews 6:15) ESV

God is not human. God doesn't lie. If God said it, then it will happen. Being patient is essential in the Christian journey. Some blessings and promises are on the waiting list because God needs to prepare you for what He has for you, so you will be able to steward over it properly. God knows when you are ready to receive. If God gave you the blessings prematurely, then possibly you would mess it up. Although it may be delayed, doesn't mean it has been denied. God promised Abraham that He would be the father of many nations at the age of 75! Abraham didn't receive the promise until 25 years later when he was 100 years of age. Are you willing to endure to receive the promises and blessings that God has for you? Keep believing in God's promises, and in due season, they shall manifest to the glory of the Lord.

Write down what God has promised you.

Date: _____

I am grateful for…

_____

My prayer for today…

_____

_____

My song for today…

My scripture for today…

_____

My personal goals I am declaring today…

_____

Actions that I will commit to today that will align me with my personal goals…

_____

The daily affirmations that will serve me today…

_____

Date: _____

I am grateful for...

My prayer for today...

My song for today...

My scripture for today...

My personal goals I am declaring today...

Actions that I will commit to today that will align me with my personal goals...

The daily affirmations that will serve me today...

I am grateful for...

My prayer for today...

My song for today...

My scripture for today...

My personal goals I am declaring today...

Actions that I will commit to today that will align me with my personal goals...

The daily affirmations that will serve me today...

You Are
Not RESPONSIBLE
For How
Others Receive
You!

-Yves-Andre Innocent

Date: _____

I am grateful for...

_____
o _____
o _____

My prayer for today...

_____
_____
_____

My song for today...

_____
o _____

My scripture for today...

_____
_____
_____

My personal goals I am declaring today...

_____
o _____
o _____

Actions that I will commit to today that will align me with my personal goals...

_____
o _____

The daily affirmations that will serve me today...

_____
o _____
o _____

I am grateful for...

My prayer for today...

My song for today...

My scripture for today...

My personal goals I am declaring today...

Actions that I will commit to today that will align me with my personal goals...

The daily affirmations that will serve me today...

Date: _____

I am grateful for...

My prayer for today...

My song for today...

My scripture for today...

My personal goals I am declaring today...

Actions that I will commit to today that will align me with my personal goals...

The daily affirmations that will serve me today...

I am grateful for...

My prayer for today...

My song for today...

My scripture for today...

My personal goals I am declaring today...

Actions that I will commit to today that will align me with my personal goals...

The daily affirmations that will serve me today...

Weekly Self-Reflection
Practice 5

1. Reread your journal entry.
   Describe the emotions and thoughts that are present during and after your reading.

2. Describe at least one distraction that you may have encountered during the week. How did you handle it? Did it hold you back from staying focused on accomplishing your weekly goals?

3. What behaviors will you change from the previous week that will propel you into the new week?

Week 6

Divine Connections

66

That is, that I may be encouraged together with you while among you, each of us by the other's faith, both yours and mine.

(Hebrews 6:15) ESV

Dear Lord,

Add people in my life who compliment the steps that you have ordered for my life. Add people who will inspire transformation, healing, and spiritual growth in my life. Please remove those to whom I am not supposed to be connected. Reveal to me the things I cannot see. Reveal to me who I need to walk away from. Remove the toxicity that is hindering me from connecting to those who are divinely designed to be in my circle, in the name of Jesus, Amen.

Date: _____

I am grateful for...
_____
. . . .

My prayer for today...
_____
. . . .
. . . .

My song for today...
_____
. . . .

My scripture for today...
_____
. . . .

My personal goals I am declaring today...
_____
. . . .
. . . .

Actions that I will commit to today that will align me with my personal goals...
_____
. . . .
. . . .

The daily affirmations that will serve me today...
_____
. . . .

I am grateful for...

My prayer for today...

My song for today...

My scripture for today...

My personal goals I am declaring today...

Actions that I will commit to today that will align me with my personal goals...

The daily affirmations that will serve me today...

I am grateful for...

My prayer for today...

My song for today...

My scripture for today...

My personal goals I am declaring today...

Actions that I will commit to today that will align me with my personal goals...

The daily affirmations that will serve me today...

Do Not
Let Anyone BULLY
You Out of What
GOD Has For You!

Date: _____

I am grateful for...

My prayer for today...

My song for today...

My scripture for today...

My personal goals I am declaring today...

Actions that I will commit to today that will align me with my personal goals...

The daily affirmations that will serve me today...

Date: _____

I am grateful for...

My prayer for today...

My song for today...

My scripture for today...

My personal goals I am declaring today...

Actions that I will commit to today that will align me with my personal goals...

The daily affirmations that will serve me today...

Date: _____

I am grateful for…

My prayer for today…

My song for today…

My scripture for today…

My personal goals I am declaring today…

Actions that I will commit to today that will align me with my personal goals…

The daily affirmations that will serve me today…

Date: _____

I am grateful for...

___
o
⋮

My prayer for today...

___
⋮

My song for today...

___
o

My scripture for today...

___
⋮

My personal goals I am declaring today...

___
o
⋮

Actions that I will commit to today that will align me with my personal goals...

___
o
o

The daily affirmations that will serve me today...

___
o

Weekly Self-Reflection
Practice 6

1 Reread your journal entry.
Describe the emotions and thoughts that are present during and after your reading.

....

....

....

2 Describe at least one distraction that you may have encountered during the week. How did you handle it? Did it hold you back from staying focused on accomplishing your weekly goals?

....

....

....

3 What behaviors will you change from the previous week that will propel you into the new week?

....

....

Self-Reflection
Prompts

01. God and nature speak to me … _____

2. Questions that I would like to ask God are…

3. Qualities and characteristics of people I should be connected to are…

4. Before I enter a relationship, business deal, and/or position, I will…

5. I show myself love by … _____

6. One thing that I would do if I knew I would never fail would be…

7. Practices that I employ or will employ that assist me into entering the next realm of my purpose are...

8. I give myself grace by...

9. I forgive myself for...

10. I apologize to myself for....

11. I am proud of myself for...

12. What makes me smile is...

13. The risks I am willing to take are...

You Owe YOURSELF The Best Version Of Yourself

Write a letter to your future self.

Five years from now.

Date/Time: _____

Dear.........................

....

....

....

....

....

....

....

....

....

....

....

....

....

....

....

....

....

....

....

....